# DRAW IT!

ARCTURUS

ARCTURUS

This edition published in 2012 by Arcturus Publishing Limited
26/27 Bickels Yard, 151–153 Bermondsey Street,
London SE1 3HA

ISBN: 978-1-84858-132-6
CH002151US
Supplier 05, Date 0712, Print Run 1378

Printed in Singapore

# Contents

Introduction ............................................ 4

Animals ................................................ 8

Speed Machines ................................ 24

Dinosaurs ........................................... 38

Sports People .................................... 52

Bugs .................................................... 66

Fantasy Figures ................................ 82

Pets ..................................................... 98

Sea Creatures ................................. 112

# Introduction

This book will teach you how to draw pictures of lots of different things. You may have thought some of them were too difficult to even try!

Our artists have lots of clever ways to help you to draw things. Follow the stages, step-by-step, and we can share them with you!

① First choose a photograph of the subject you want to draw.

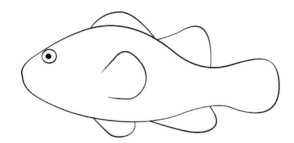

② Begin by drawing basic outline shapes.

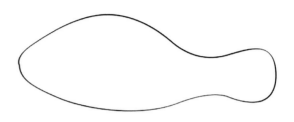

③ Add in a bit more detail. At this stage your subject should start to become recognizable.

④ Add in the final details to complete your line drawing.

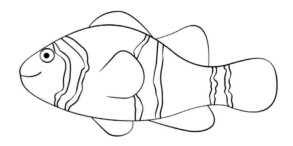

⑤ Color in your drawing to match the photograph, or pick your own colors.

# Materials

Before we start, let's get some materials together.

Gather up your pencils, pens and paintbrushes. Make sure your pencils are sharp!

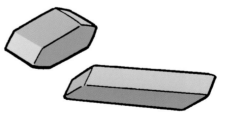

You can use any smooth, white paper to practice your pencil drawing. Spend some time practicing on cheap paper to build up your confidence, saving the nicer paper for your final drawing. If you're going to colour your drawing, start with a strong watercolour paper that will resist wrinkling.

An eraser with a chisel-shaped end is ideal for correcting and removing small bits of your drawing. Use a big, soft eraser after inking to remove all the rough pencil lines.

Compasses draw the best circles.

Sometimes we need lines to be very straight and neat. Using a ruler will help with this.

# Inking and Coloring

The drawings in this book have been finished with an ink line. You can apply ink with a a special felt tip, dipping pen or even a fine brush. The ink must be waterproof if you are going to use water-based paints to color your picture.

Color your pictures with felt tips, pencils or paint – it's up to you! If you choose paint, you can use water-based paint like poster paint or gouache.

It is important to pick the right paintbrush for your picture. Use round, pointed ones for fine detail and broad ones for flat areas of color.

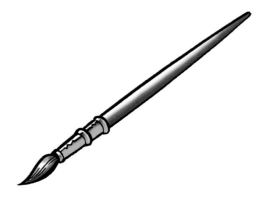

Get this tiger's snarl just right.

This snooty camel is fun to draw!

Give this polar bear a realistic looking coat.

Copy and color this proud lion.

# ANIMALS

Animals are fun to draw because they come in all shapes, sizes and colors! This chapter shows you how to draw wild animals that you may not have seen in real life before, but using photographs you can draw these cool creatures!

# Tiger

The tiger is the largest cat.

His stripes help him to hide in the trees. Most tigers have more than 100 stripes.

He has long front teeth for biting.

He has strong paws with long claws.

FUN FACTS ● FUN FACTS ● FUN FACTS ● FUN FACTS ● FUN FACTS

Most tigers are orange with black stripes.
However, some tigers are white with black stripes!

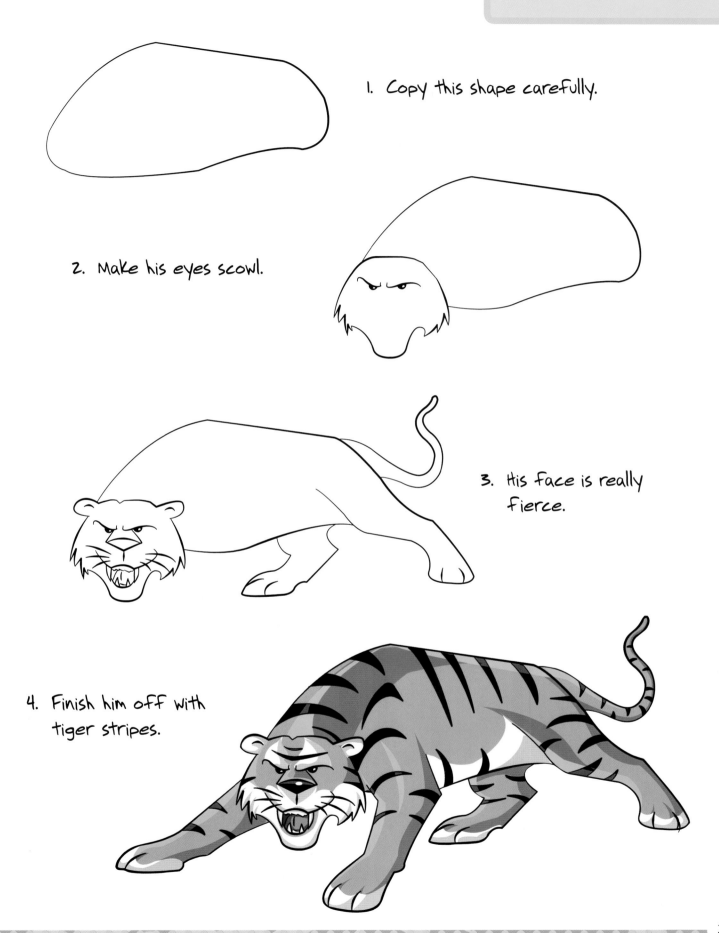

1. Copy this shape carefully.

2. Make his eyes scowl.

3. His face is really fierce.

4. Finish him off with tiger stripes.

# Giraffe

The giraffe is the tallest animal.

Giraffes have spots on their coats. Each giraffe has a different spotty pattern.

She eats leaves from tall trees.

Giraffes sleep for two hours each day. Sometimes they nap standing up.

FUN FACTS ● FUN FACTS ● FUN FACTS ● FUN FACTS ● FUN FACTS

A father giraffe is called a bull. A mother is called a cow. A baby is called a calf!

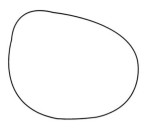

1. Her body is quite small.

2. Make her neck long and curvy.

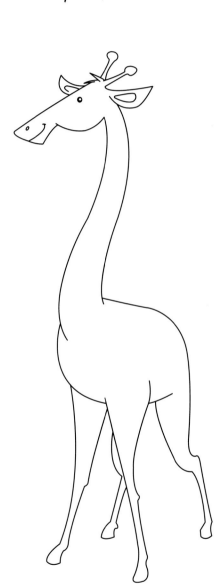

4. She has a special pattern on her coat.

3. Give her four strong legs.

# Lion

A lion has thick hair around his neck. This is called a mane.

The lion hunts other animals for food. He has excellent eyesight.

A lion is about as long as a man lying down.

His claws are very sharp.

FUN FACTS ● FUN FACTS ● FUN FACTS ● FUN FACTS ● FUN FACTS

Lions roar to communicate with each other. A lion's roar can be heard 5 miles (8 km away. That's loud!

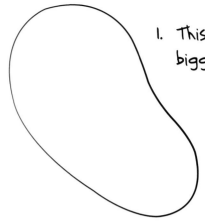

1. This is the body. He's bigger at the front.

2. He has long hair all around his face.

3. Make his jaws big and strong.

4. Don't forget the brush on the end of his tail!

# Orangutan

Orangutans like to swing between trees.

An orangutan's arms are long and strong.

She has long fingers. They can hold on tight to branches.

All orangutans have reddish-brown or orange hair.

FUN FACTS ● FUN FACTS ● FUN FACTS ● FUN FACTS ● FUN FACTS

Orangutans are very smart. They can even learn to use sign language.

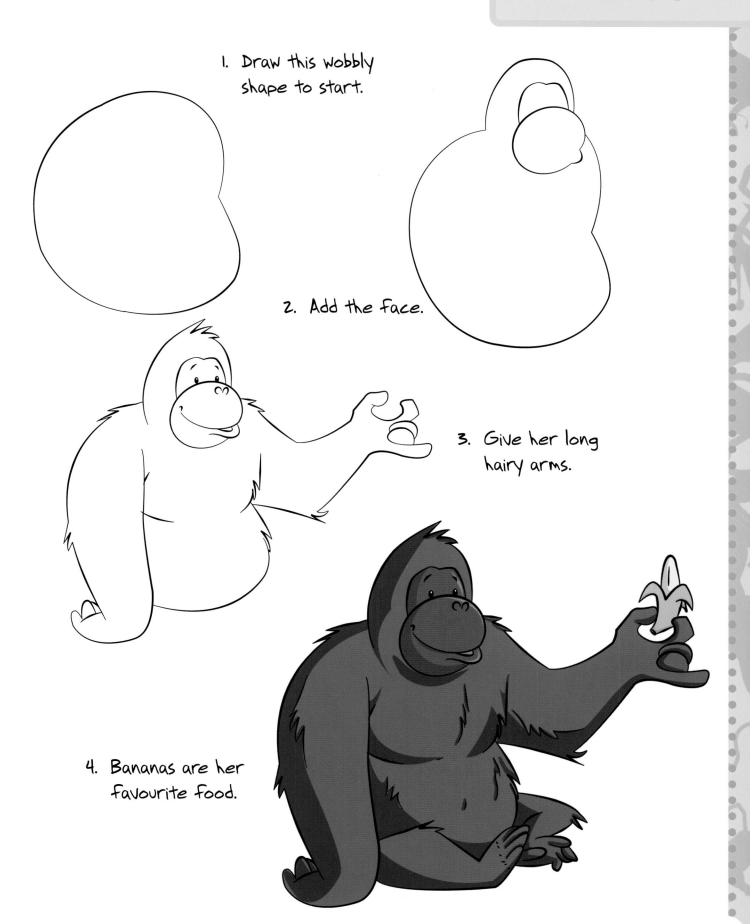

1. Draw this wobbly shape to start.

2. Add the face.

3. Give her long hairy arms.

4. Bananas are her favourite food.

# Camel

Long eyelashes protect the camel's eyes from sand.

His hump stores fat.

This camel has one hump, but some types have two humps.

He has wide, padded feet for walking on soft sand.

FUN FACTS ● FUN FACTS ● FUN FACTS ● FUN FACTS ● FUN FACTS

If a camel doesn't eat for a while, the fat in its hump is used up. The hump goes all floppy!

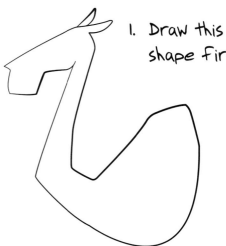

1. Draw this shape first.

2. Now put in a front and a back leg.

3. Add the other legs.

4. He's got a hairy hump and a hairy chin.

# Polar Bear

The polar bear is the biggest meat eater on land.

His claws help him to catch animals. They also stop him falling over on the ice.

He lives in the far north. It is very cold there. His fur keeps him warm.

His fur is white, like the snow.

FUN FACTS ● FUN FACTS ● FUN FACTS ● FUN FACTS ● FUN FACTS

Under the polar bear's white fur, it has black skin!

1. Draw the body like a big teardrop.

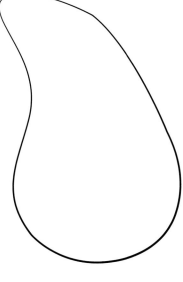

2. He looks as if he's growling.

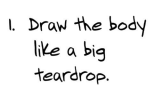

3. Give him sharp claws and teeth.

4. He's standing on his back legs, ready to fight!

# Elephant

He has a long, curly tooth called a tusk.

The elephant flaps his ears to keep cool.

He uses his long trunk like a hand for picking things up.

He needs thick, strong legs because he is so heavy.

FUN FACTS ● FUN FACTS ● FUN FACTS ● FUN FACTS ● FUN FACTS

The elephant is the largest animal that lives on land.
It weighs 9 tons (8,000 kg).

1. Begin with a big egg shape.

2. Put in his mouth and his curly trunk ...

3. ... ears, tusks and some legs.

4. Color him gray and don't forget his tail!

Use clean
lines on this
sleek fighter.

This speedboat
will skim through
the water.

All aboard this
super-fast
bullet train!

Have fun
designing your
own F1 car!

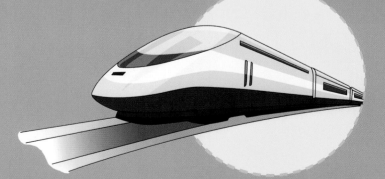

# SPEED MACHINES

Become a vehicle drawing pro, down to the last nut and bolt! But you'd better hurry, before these supercharged speed machines race away!

# Racing car

A racing car has a powerful engine.

The back wing helps to keep the car on the road.

This car is very light but strong.

The tyres are very wide. This stops the car from skidding.

FUN FACTS ● FUN FACTS ● FUN FACTS ● FUN FACTS ● FUN FACTS

The controls of the car are all on the steering wheel. The driver can find them quickly and easily.

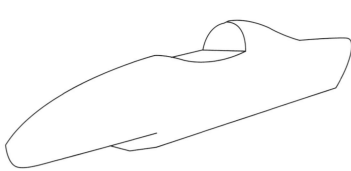

1. First, copy this smooth shape.

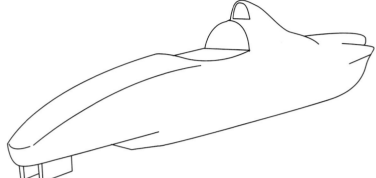

2. Add these shapes behind the driver's seat and at the front of the car.

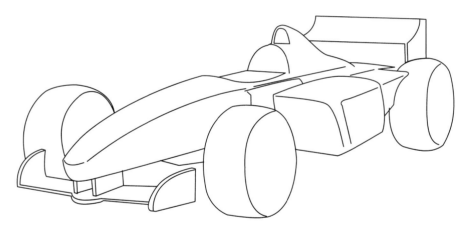

3. Now add some wheels, and the wings at the front and back.

4. Red is a good color for a racing car.

# Fighter plane

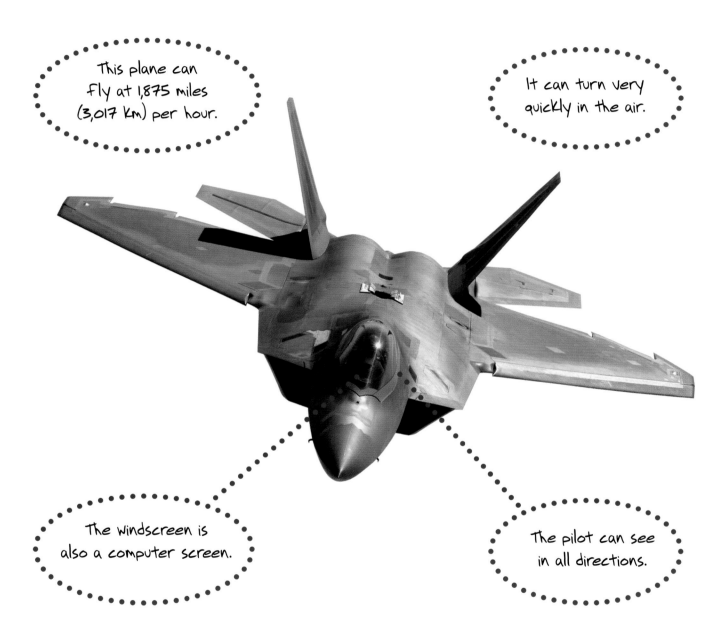

This plane can fly at 1,875 miles (3,017 km) per hour.

It can turn very quickly in the air.

The windscreen is also a computer screen.

The pilot can see in all directions.

FUN FACTS ● FUN FACTS ● FUN FACTS ● FUN FACTS ● FUN FACTS

Fighter pilots must be super fit to withstand the pressures that the g-forces place on their bodies.

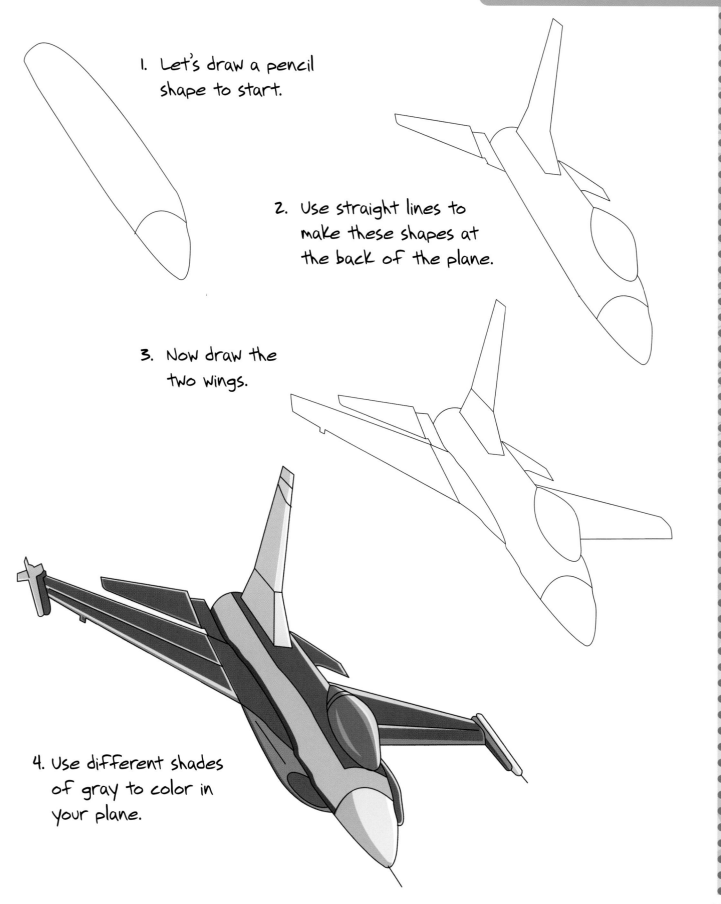

1. Let's draw a pencil shape to start.

2. Use straight lines to make these shapes at the back of the plane.

3. Now draw the two wings.

4. Use different shades of gray to color in your plane.

# Quad Bike

The driver steers the quad bike with handlebars, like a motorcycle.

Quad bikes can be driven over very bumpy ground.

They can travel at 70 miles (112 km) per hour.

They have four wheels so they don't tip over.

FUN FACTS ● FUN FACTS ● FUN FACTS ● FUN FACTS ● FUN FACTS

Quad bike races take place on roads, over grass, on sand and even on ice!

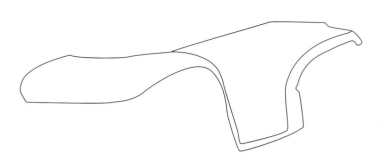

1. Draw the top of the quad bike first.

2. Now put in the headlights and the seat.

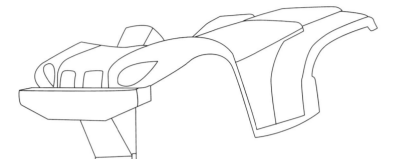

3. Put in the wheels next.

4. It has fat tyres for driving over muddy fields.

# Speedboat

The windshield protects the pilot from the air rushing over the boat.

The powerful engine is at the back of the boat.

The front of the speedboat lifts up so it isn't touching the water.

011

FUN FACTS ● FUN FACTS ● FUN FACTS ● FUN FACTS ● FUN FACTS

The world record for the fastest speed on water is 317 miles (510 km) per hour. This record was set in 1978.

1. Draw the top and one side. Make the front pointed so that it can cut through the air easily.

2. Add these shapes next.

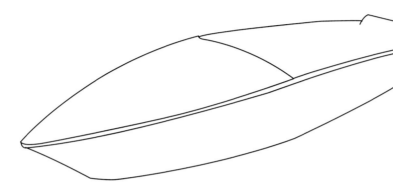

3. The windshield goes at the front.

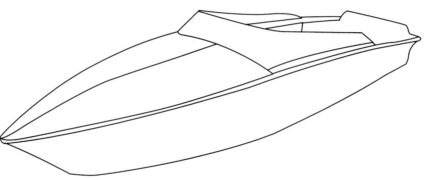

4. Finish off the windshield and add an engine at the back.

# Bullet train

The front of this train is long and thin. This helps it to go faster.

The train is powered by electricity.

The fastest bullet trains reach speeds of 200 miles (322 km) per hour.

The train has a smooth shape. It can slip through the air easily.

FUN FACTS ● FUN FACTS ● FUN FACTS ● FUN FACTS ● FUN FACTS

It is possible to build faster bullet trains, but they are too noisy to use.

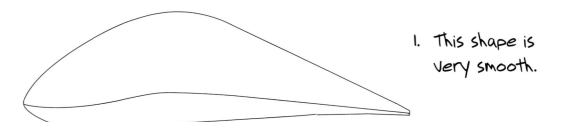

1. This shape is very smooth.

2. Draw the big windshield at the front. Show where the carriages join together.

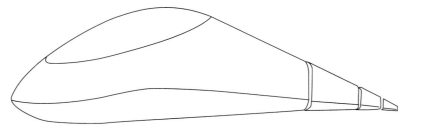

3. Don't forget the rails.

4. Now color in your train.

# Sports car

The roof folds away with the press of a button.

This bar can carry the weight of the car if it rolls over in a crash.

There is only space for two people in this car.

These holes take air to the engine to help it work.

FUN FACTS ● FUN FACTS ● FUN FACTS ● FUN FACTS ● FUN FACTS

This car has a top speed of almost 200 miles (322 km) per hour.

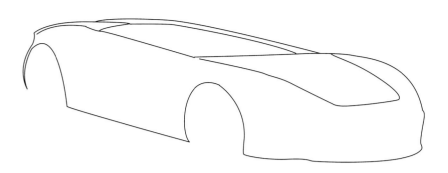

1. This car shape is very curved.

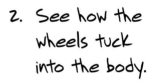

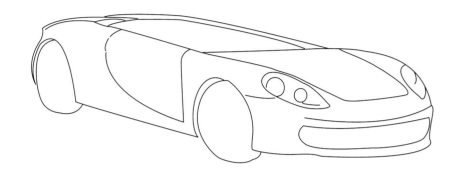

2. See how the wheels tuck into the body.

3. Add the windshield and the passenger seat.

4. Now your car is ready to color in.

Draw this Triceratops, with his famous three horns.

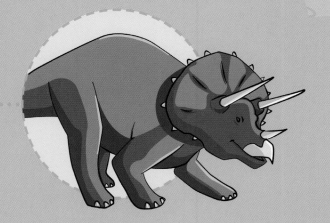

Velociraptor was a fast runner with sharp claws.

T. rex is on the hunt for his next meal!

Brachiosaurus had a tiny head compared to his body!

# DINOSAURS

After millions of years we are still trying to figure out what the dinosaurs really looked like! Perfect your drawing technique on these prehistoric monsters.

# Tyrannosaurus rex

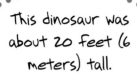

This dinosaur was about 20 feet (6 meters) tall.

Tyrannosaurus rex was one of the biggest meat eaters there has ever been.

It had very sharp teeth.

Its powerful legs helped it to run very fast.

FUN FACTS ● FUN FACTS ● FUN FACTS ● FUN FACTS ● FUN FACTS

Tyrannosaurus rex was so powerful that it could crush bones with its teeth.

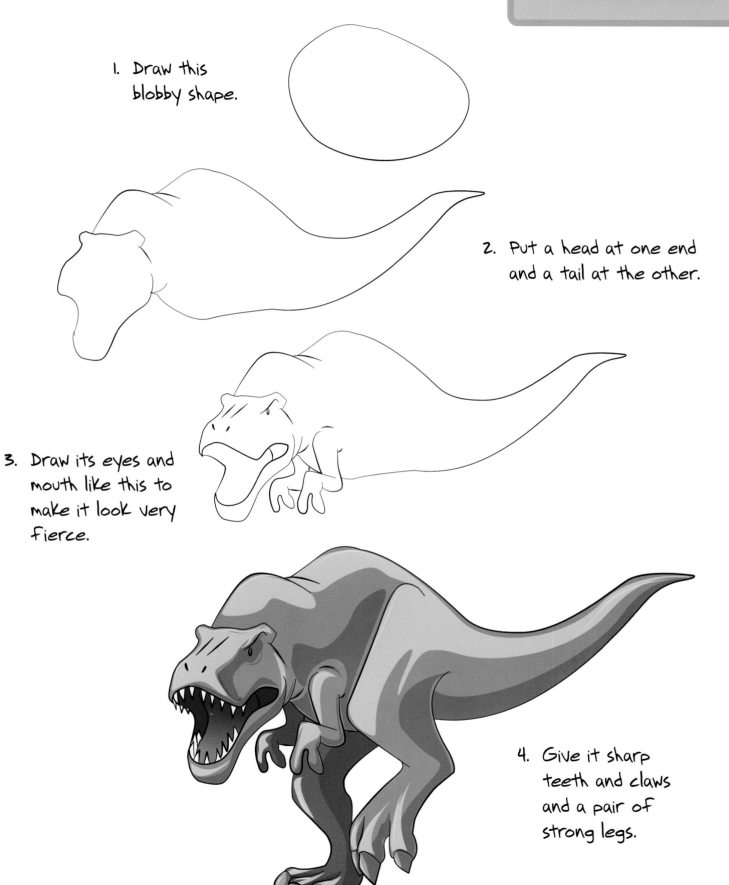

1. Draw this blobby shape.

2. Put a head at one end and a tail at the other.

3. Draw its eyes and mouth like this to make it look very fierce.

4. Give it sharp teeth and claws and a pair of strong legs.

# Pteranodon

Pteranodon lived at the same time as the dinosaurs.

It used its big wings to glide over the sea.

Its wings were tough and leathery.

It scooped up fish in its big mouth.

FUN FACTS ● FUN FACTS ● FUN FACTS ● FUN FACTS ● FUN FACTS

From wing to wing, Pteranodon was nearly 25 feet (8 meters) wide.

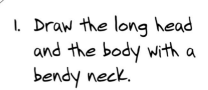

1. Draw the long head and the body with a bendy neck.

2. Add one big wing.

3. Put in the other wing and a tiny leg.

4. Give it another leg and put a smile on its face.

# Triceratops

Triceratops was about 30 feet (9 meters) long.

This dinosaur had two large horns and one smaller horn.

It ate leaves and twigs.

It had strong legs to support its heavy body.

FUN FACTS ● FUN FACTS ● FUN FACTS ● FUN FACTS ● FUN FACTS

Triceratops had a bony plate around its neck to protect it from big meat eaters.

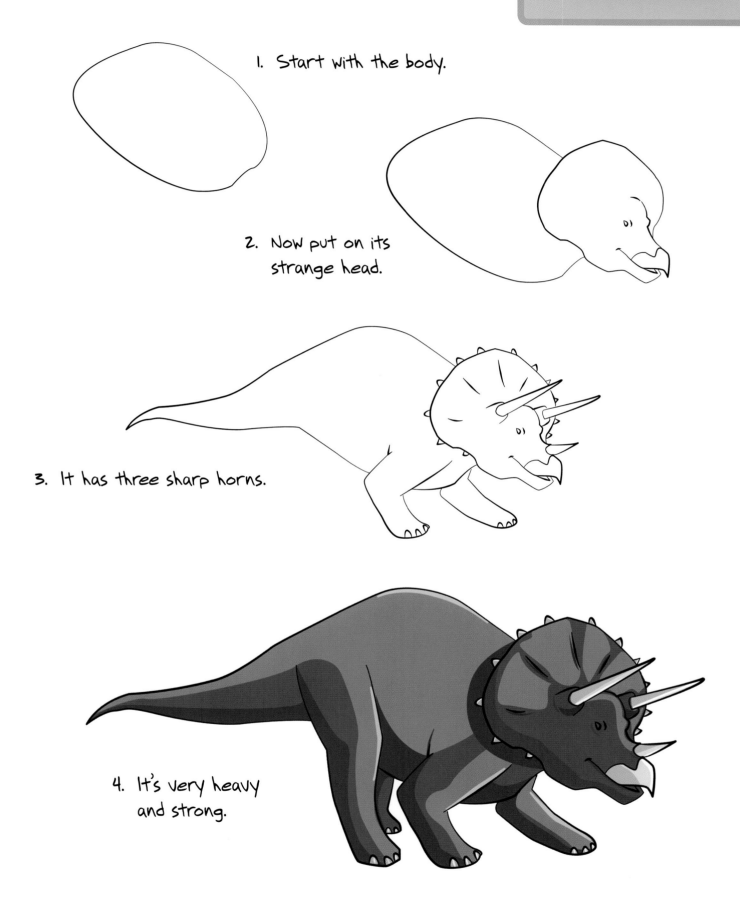

1. Start with the body.

2. Now put on its strange head.

3. It has three sharp horns.

4. It's very heavy and strong.

# Stegosaurus

This dinosaur ate plants that grew near the ground.

Stegosaurus was about 30 feet (9 meters) long.

It had sharp spikes on its tail to protect itself.

Its front legs were much shorter than its back legs.

FUN FACTS ● FUN FACTS ● FUN FACTS ● FUN FACTS ● FUN FACTS

Stegosaurus had a very small brain. It was only about the size of a walnut.

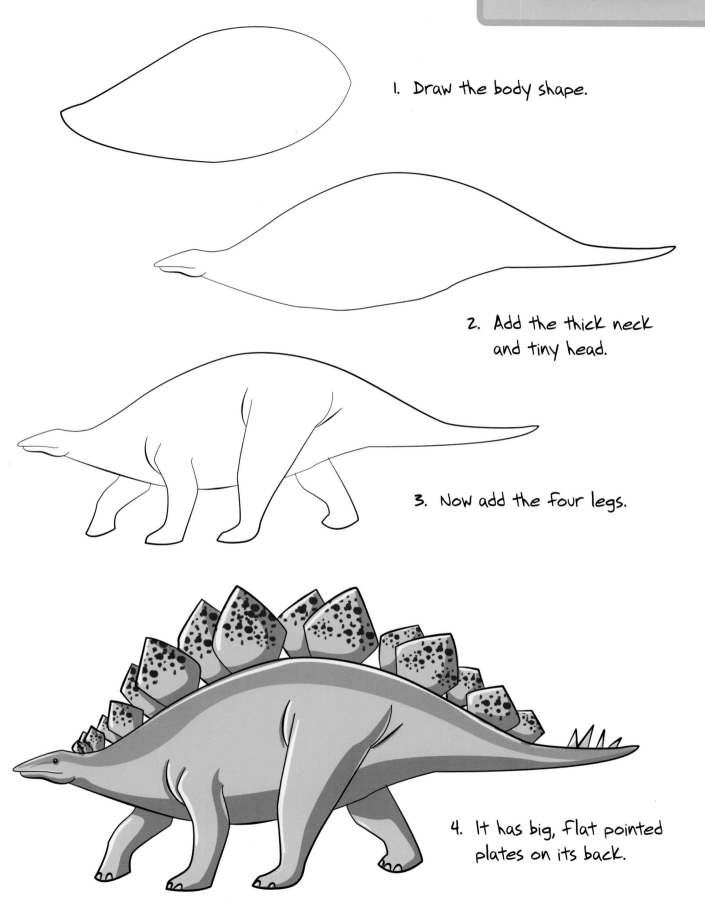

1. Draw the body shape.

2. Add the thick neck and tiny head.

3. Now add the four legs.

4. It has big, flat pointed plates on its back.

# Velociraptor

This dinosaur was a fierce meat eater.

Its long legs made it a fast runner.

It had long claws on its back feet.

Its front claws were very sharp to grab prey.

FUN FACTS ● FUN FACTS ● FUN FACTS ● FUN FACTS ● FUN FACTS

A fossil has been found of a Velociraptor attacking a plant-eating dinosaur called Protoceratops.

1. Here's the body.

2. Draw the neck and a long, pointy tail.

3. The head and the back legs are next.

4. Put in its front legs and its sharp teeth.

# Brachiosaurus

It used its long neck to reach the leaves at the top of trees.

This huge dinosaur was 75 feet (23 meters) long.

It swallowed food without chewing it.

Its front legs were longer than its back legs.

FUN FACTS ● FUN FACTS ● FUN FACTS ● FUN FACTS ● FUN FACTS

A meat-eating dinosaur would not attack an adult Brachiosaurus. It was just too big!

1. A bumpy egg is the starting place for this dinosaur.

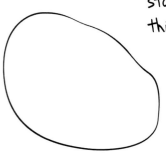

2. Give it a long neck and tail.

3. It has thick and powerful front legs.

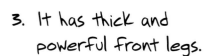

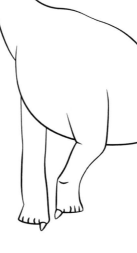

4. Short back legs help keep this dinosaur on its feet.

This flexible gymnast is striking a pose.

Draw this baseball player scoring a home run!

Where do you think this cool dude is skating?

This windsurfer is racing across the water!

# SPORTS PEOPLE

People can be hard to draw, especially when they're moving! Improve your figure drawing skills by practicing with these sports people in action poses.

# Skateboarder

A skater can do tricks. He makes the board jump into the air.

Skateboards can go very fast!

He wears skate shoes and baggy clothes. These clothes let him move easily.

The top of the skateboard is rough. It helps the skater stay on.

FUN FACTS ● FUN FACTS ● FUN FACTS ● FUN FACTS ● FUN FACTS

Skateboarding was started by surfers. They wanted something to do when there were no waves!

1. Draw a head with a hat and a body.

2. Put in two strong legs.

3. Add his arms to help him balance.

4. Finish off with some pads on his elbows and knees.

# Windsurfer

The wind blows the windsurfer across the water.

He has to know where the wind is coming from.

The sail traps the wind. It pushes the board along.

A windsurfer can do tricks. He can also take part in races.

FUN FACTS ● FUN FACTS ● FUN FACTS ● FUN FACTS ● FUN FACTS

Some people windsurf on indoor pools. Big fans make the wind!

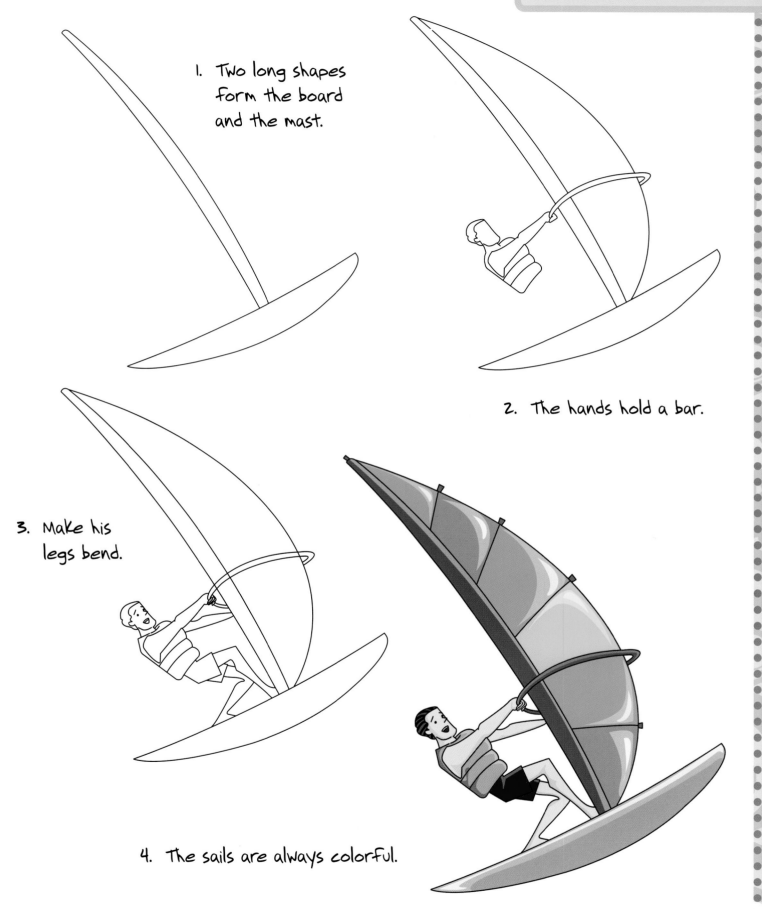

1. Two long shapes form the board and the mast.

2. The hands hold a bar.

3. Make his legs bend.

4. The sails are always colorful.

# Ballet dancer

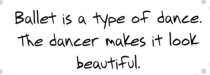

Ballet is a type of dance. The dancer makes it look beautiful.

The dancer needs strong arms and legs.

This ballet skirt is called a tutu.

She dances on the tips of her toes.

FUN FACTS ● FUN FACTS ● FUN FACTS ● FUN FACTS ● FUN FACTS

Dancers wear out ballet shoes very quickly. Some dancers get through two pairs each week!

1. Draw her graceful body and pretty skirt.

2. Her hair is put up in a bun.

3. Her arms are held out wide to help her balance.

4. She balances tall on one leg.

# Soccer player

A soccer player plays on a team. There are 11 people in his team.

He can't touch the ball with his hands or arms.

Each team has a color. The player wears it on his shirt and shorts.

Special soccer boots help him to run and kick.

FUN FACTS ● FUN FACTS ● FUN FACTS ● FUN FACTS ● FUN FACTS

Soccer is the most popular ball game in the world.

1. Draw the body first.

2. Put on his head and arms.

3. He is running fast.

4. Don't forget the ball!

# Baseball player

A baseball player wears a cap. It keeps the sun out of his eyes.

This player is a hitter. He holds a baseball bat.

His uniform shows the colours of his team.

The player who throws the ball is called the pitcher.

FUN FACTS ● FUN FACTS ● FUN FACTS ● FUN FACTS ● FUN FACTS

The longest baseball game ever lasted eight hours!

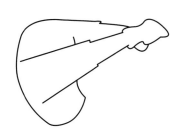

1. Draw his arms and the top of his body.

2. Add his head.

3. Put in his long legs.

4. He's just hit the ball!

# Gymnast

In gymnastics, people do special exercises.

The moves are hard. She makes them look easy.

She must practice every day.

She stands on one leg to do this exercise.

FUN FACTS ● FUN FACTS ● FUN FACTS ● FUN FACTS ● FUN FACTS

The first gymnasts lived in Greece more than two thousand years ago!

1. This shape is the body and the head.

2. One arm is reaching up.

3. She balances on her toes.

4. Her other leg is raised high behind her.

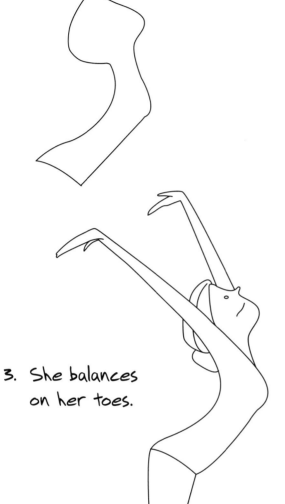

# BUGS

Get down to ground level and take a look around – there are hundreds of amazing bugs and minibeasts all around your feet! These bugs are colorful and fun to draw.

# Caterpillar

This caterpillar eats leaves. He grows very fast.

When he gets too big for his old skin, he will wriggle out of it. There is a new, bigger skin underneath.

He can hang from a silk thread that comes out of his mouth.

He has a long, round body and lots of legs.

FUN FACTS ● FUN FACTS ● FUN FACTS ● FUN FACTS ● FUN FACTS

Caterpillars hatch out of eggs. Later they will turn into butterflies or moths.

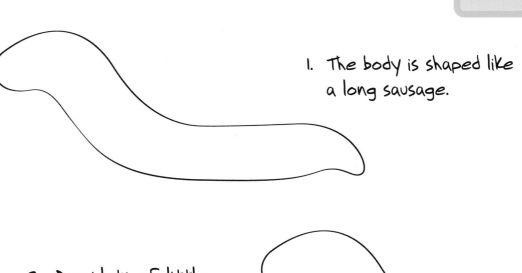

1. The body is shaped like a long sausage.

2. Draw lots of little legs along the bottom of the body.

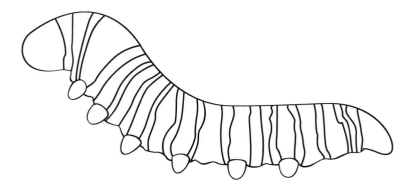

3. Add plenty of stripes to make him stand out.

4. Lots of bright colors and long antennae finish off this happy caterpillar.

# Snail

This snail's eyes are at the top of her two biggest feelers.

She can tuck her body inside her shell if she is in danger.

The shorter feelers are used for smelling.

She has no legs and moves slowly on her soft body.

FUN FACTS ● FUN FACTS ● FUN FACTS ● FUN FACTS ● FUN FACTS

Snails leave a trail of slime behind them. The slime makes it easier for them to move.

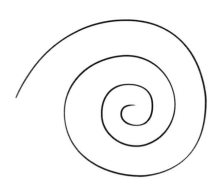

1. Start with a simple spiral.

2. Draw in a slug-shaped body.

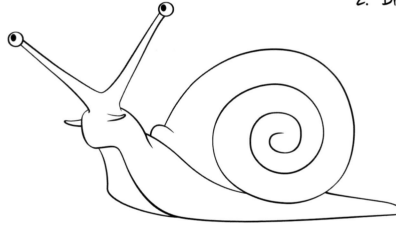

3. Add her feelers and her eyes.

4. Don't forget the slime trail when you color her in.

# Butterfly

Her mouth is like a straw. She drinks nectar from flowers.

This butterfly is a beautiful blue color.

She flies in the day, not at night.

She has a long, thin, smooth body.

FUN FACTS ● FUN FACTS ● FUN FACTS ● FUN FACTS ● FUN FACTS

One type of butterfly travels from Canada to Mexico, a journey of over 2,000 miles (3,200 km).

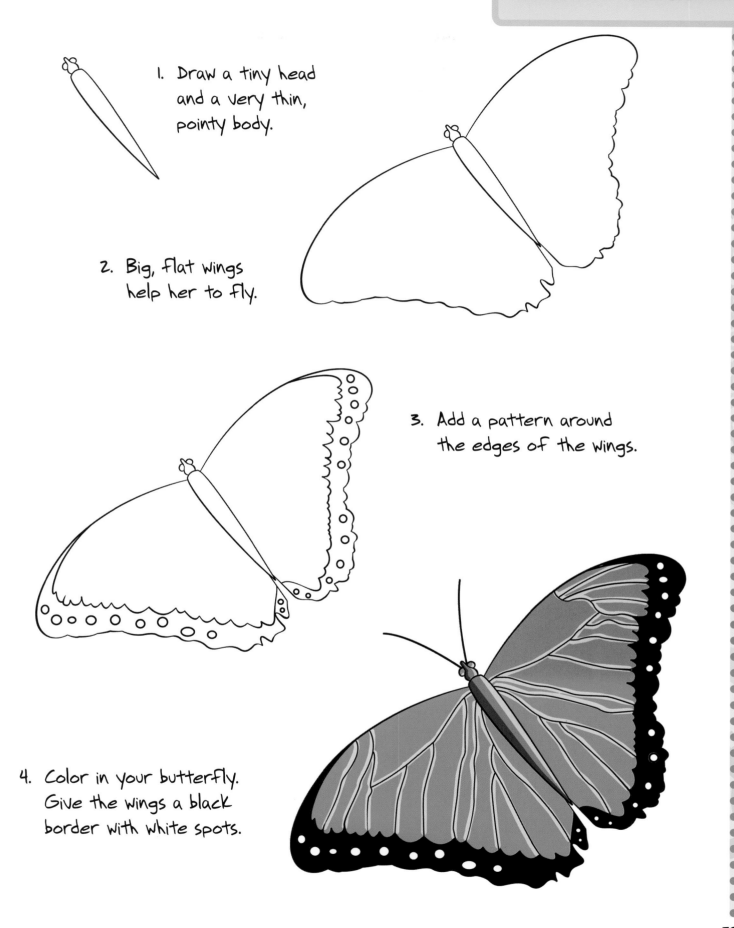

1. Draw a tiny head and a very thin, pointy body.

2. Big, flat wings help her to fly.

3. Add a pattern around the edges of the wings.

4. Color in your butterfly. Give the wings a black border with white spots.

# Ladybug

This ladybug is red with seven black spots.

Her wings are under her hard back.

She eats small, soft insects such as aphids.

She has six legs.

FUN FACTS ● FUN FACTS ● FUN FACTS ● FUN FACTS ● FUN FACTS

In the autumn, ladybugs gather together in a safe, sheltered spot. They sleep through the winter.

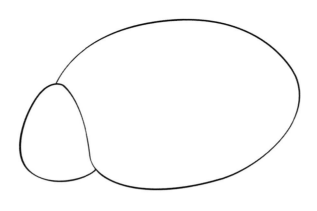

1. Draw two squashed circles for the body and the head.

2. Divide the head and body with simple lines.

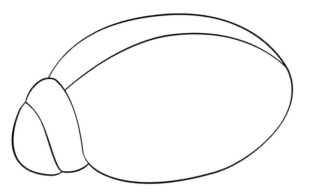

3. Add some short legs. The ladybug has six legs, but you can only see four in this picture.

4. Color her bright red and add black spots.

# Stag beetle

He has big jaws that he uses to fight other males.

This stag beetle has a hard body.

Female stag beetles are smaller than males. They do not have big jaws.

He has wings. They are hidden under here.

FUN FACTS ● FUN FACTS ● FUN FACTS ● FUN FACTS ● FUN FACTS

Stag beetles lay their eggs in old wood. Young beetles live in the wood or under the ground for several years.

1. Two squashed circles and one long oval make the head and body.

2. Add his huge jaws at the front.

3. Draw legs that get thinner at the ends.

4. Finish off by coloring him brown and black.

# Dragonfly

This dragonfly has four wings. She's a very good flier.

She has a brightly colored body.

She has huge eyes.

She catches her food with her front two legs.

FUN FACTS ● FUN FACTS ● FUN FACTS ● FUN FACTS ● FUN FACTS

Young dragonflies live underwater for several years. Only the adult dragonfly has wings and can fly.

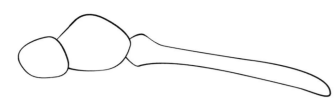

1. Draw these shapes to make the head and body.

2. Add some legs. Dragonflies have six legs, but you can only see four in this picture.

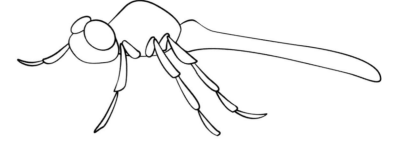

3. Draw four long, narrow wings.

4. Color the wings pale blue to make them appear see-through.

# Bumblebee

She is brightly colored, with black and yellow stripes.

She has a sting at the end of her body.

This bumblebee lives with lots of other bees in a nest under the ground.

She is covered in hair to keep her warm.

FUN FACTS ● FUN FACTS ● FUN FACTS ● FUN FACTS ● FUN FACTS

Bees move their wings very fast. Their wings make a buzzing noise when they fly.

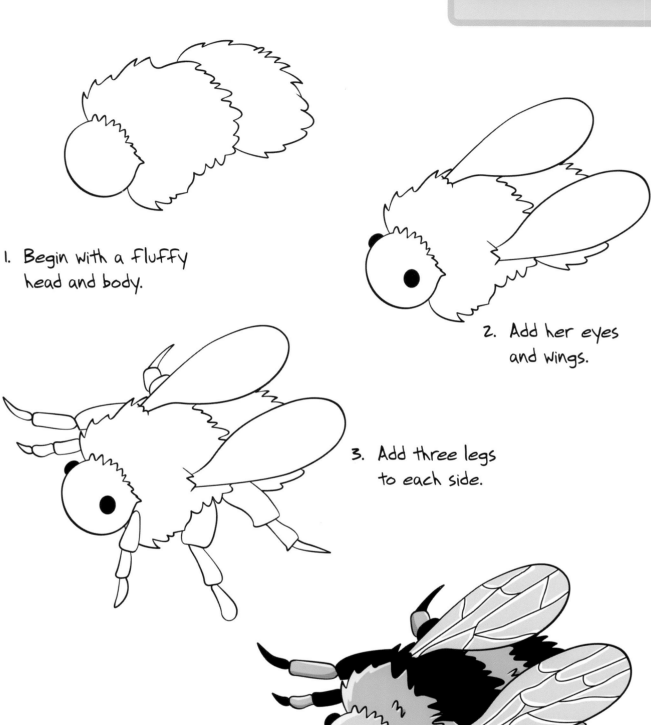

1. Begin with a fluffy head and body.

2. Add her eyes and wings.

3. Add three legs to each side.

4. Use black and yellow to color her body and pale blue to make her wings look light and thin.

Hubble bubble, this wicked witch spells trouble!

This moving mummy is fun to draw!

Try drawing this pretty mermaid.

What spell is this wizard going to cast?

# FANTASY FIGURES

Let your imagination run wild in this chapter! It's filled with mysterious, magical creatures. Whether you like monstrous mummies or fluttering fairies, there are lots of fantastic things to draw in here!

# Fairy

In stories, a fairy is a magical creature.

Fairies can fly. This one has wings like a butterfly.

She looks like a person, only she is very tiny.

Fairies are helpful and kind to people.

FUN FACTS ● FUN FACTS ● FUN FACTS ● FUN FACTS ● FUN FACTS

In books and movies, one of the most famous fairies is Tinker Bell. She is the friend of Peter Pan.

1. Start with the slim body.

2. Now draw her head and her hair.

3. Put in her arms and her legs.

4. Add the wings so she can fly!

# Wizard

This wizard is old and wise. He has a long beard.

He is wearing a pointed hat. It has a moon and a star on it.

He carries a magic stick called a staff.

He wears a long cape.

FUN FACTS ● FUN FACTS ● FUN FACTS ● FUN FACTS ● FUN FACTS

Not all wizards are old. One of the most famous wizards is a schoolboy called Harry Potter!

1. Draw the body first.

2. Now put in his pointy hat and his pointy beard.

3. Finish his face and draw in his arms.

4. In his hand he's holding his magic staff.

# Pirate

Pirates sail across the sea in pirate ships. They steal from other ships.

This pirate has a big, black pirate hat.

A pirate needs to be good at sailing and fighting.

Many pirates were injured in fights.

FUN FACTS ● FUN FACTS ● FUN FACTS ● FUN FACTS ● FUN FACTS

Pirate ships flew a flag called the Jolly Roger. It showed a picture of a skull with two crossed bones!

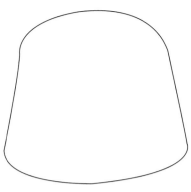

1. His body is shaped like a barrel.

2. On top you can draw his hat.

3. The best pirates have eyepatches.

4. He's got one eye, one hand and one leg. Yo ho ho!

# Mermaid

She has long hair. Mermaids often carry a comb and a mirror.

In stories, a mermaid is half human and half fish.

A creature with a man's body and a fish's tail is called a merman.

She has a girl's body and a fish's tail.

FUN FACTS ● FUN FACTS ● FUN FACTS ● FUN FACTS ● FUN FACTS

Long ago, sailors told stories about mermaids who sang to them. Sailors thought mermaids were bad luck!

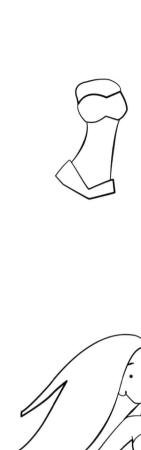

1. Here's her body.

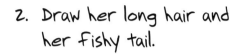

2. Draw her long hair and her fishy tail.

3. Add her face and arms.

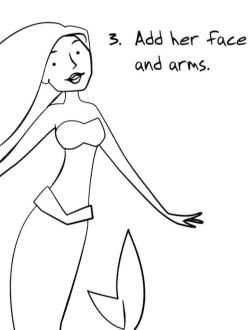

4. Put in some bubbles so we can see she's in the water.

# Mummy

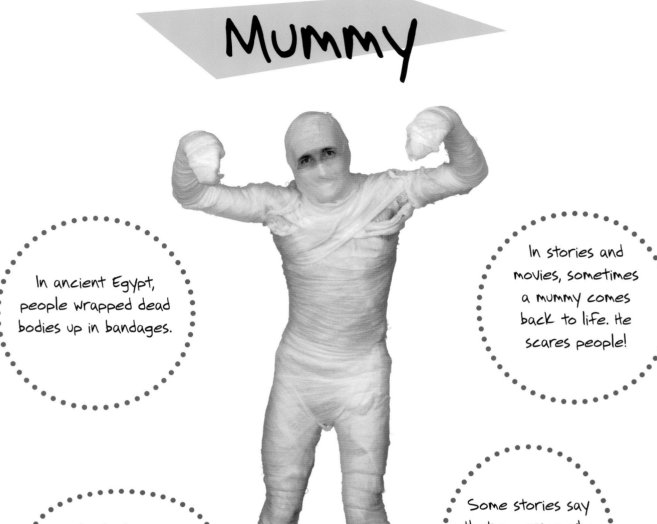

In ancient Egypt, people wrapped dead bodies up in bandages.

In stories and movies, sometimes a mummy comes back to life. He scares people!

The bodies are called mummies.

Some stories say that a person who finds a mummy will have bad luck.

FUN FACTS ● FUN FACTS ● FUN FACTS ● FUN FACTS ● FUN FACTS

In Egypt, scientists have uncovered mummies that have been buried for thousands of years!

1. Draw his head and rectangular body.

2. Give him staring eyes and make his hands reach out.

3. He's jumping at us!

4. Cover him in bandages and give him green eyes.

# Witch

She wears a pointy witch's hat.

A scary woman who does magic is called a witch.

She has a tooth missing and a wart on her nose.

She is wearing a long black dress. She has green skin!

FUN FACTS ● FUN FACTS ● FUN FACTS ● FUN FACTS ● FUN FACTS

Long ago, people thought that witches were real. If they got sick, they might think it was a witch's magic spell!

1. Here's her body.

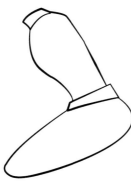

2. Draw her head and tall hat.

3. She has long messy hair.

4. She's riding through the air on a broomstick!

# Alien

An alien is a creature from another planet.

The alien looks like a bit like a person. It has big eyes and a thin body.

If aliens exist, some people think they might look like this.

An alien could look like anything at all. You can use your imagination!

FUN FACTS ● FUN FACTS ● FUN FACTS ● FUN FACTS ● FUN FACTS

Scientists are always looking for signs of alien life in space. But so far, they haven't found any!

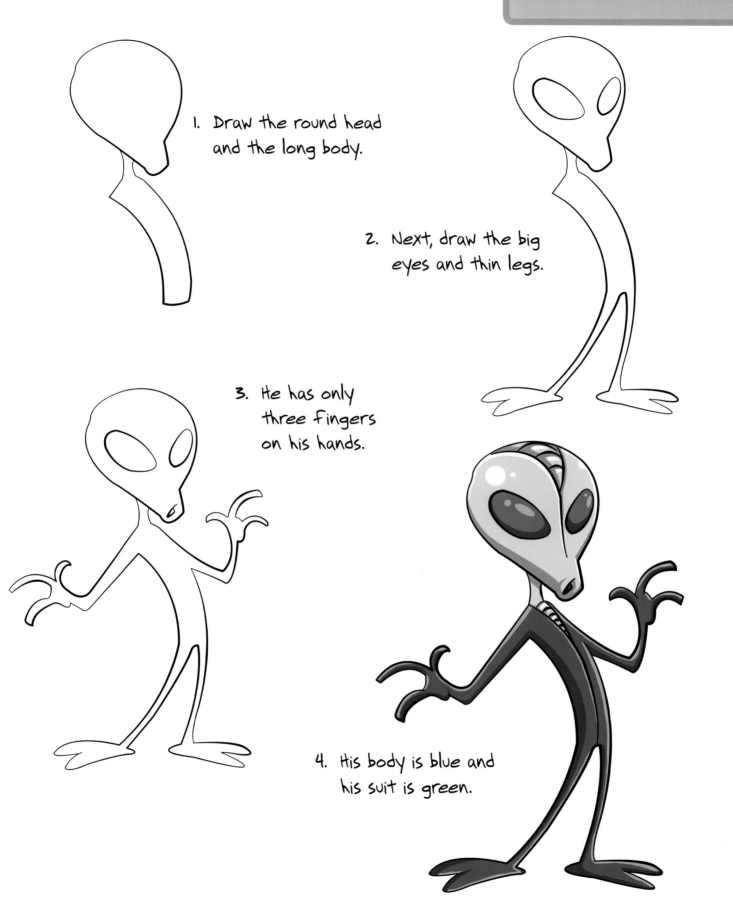

1. Draw the round head and the long body.

2. Next, draw the big eyes and thin legs.

3. He has only three fingers on his hands.

4. His body is blue and his suit is green.

Copy this tortoise's green skin and hard shell.

Learn to draw this hungry hamster.

This horse looks very pleased with himself!

Have a go at this cheeky white rabbit!

# PETS

Have a go at drawing these cute pets. With a bit of practice, you'll be doing fantastic portraits of your own furry friends in no time!

# Dog

This dog has excellent hearing.

He has a wet nose. This helps him to follow smells.

He wags his tail when he's happy.

His fur grows longer in winter.

FUN FACTS ● FUN FACTS ● FUN FACTS ● FUN FACTS ● FUN FACTS

Puppies are born with their eyes closed. They open their eyes after around two weeks!

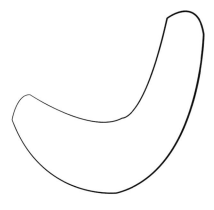

1. Start with a shape like a banana.

2. Now put on two legs and start on his head.

3. Now add his tail, the other legs and the rest of his face.

4. Add his tongue. Make his nose look shiny.

# Hamster

This hamster has two sharp front teeth.

She has pouches in her mouth. She carries food in them.

She likes digging! She uses her claws to dig.

She has long whiskers.

FUN FACTS ● FUN FACTS ● FUN FACTS ● FUN FACTS ● FUN FACTS

A mother hamster may have as many as 13 babies at once!

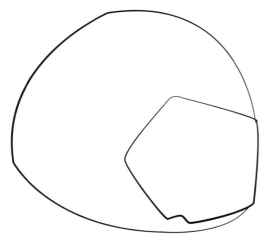

1. Here are the shapes for the head and body.

2. Draw in the face and the ears.

3. Add some little feet.

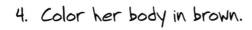

4. Color her body in brown.

# Cat

This cat's body bends easily. This helps her to jump and climb.

She can see in the dark.

She wags her tail when she's angry.

She has sharp claws.

FUN FACTS ● FUN FACTS ● FUN FACTS ● FUN FACTS ● FUN FACTS

The pet cat is the smallest type of cat. The biggest is the tiger!

1. Most of this shape is her head.

2. Make her back bend like this.

3. Her tail is a bit like a question mark.

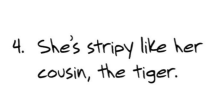

4. She's stripy like her cousin, the tiger.

# Rabbit

This rabbit has very long ears. He can hear well.

His nose twitches when he smells food.

He has strong back legs for jumping.

He stamps his feet if he's scared.

FUN FACTS ● FUN FACTS ● FUN FACTS ● FUN FACTS ● FUN FACTS

A father rabbit is called a buck. A mother rabbit is called a doe. A baby rabbit is called a kit!

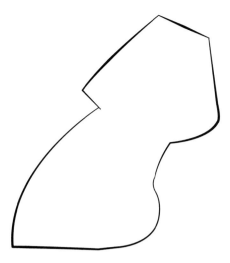

1. Start with this shape.

2. Ears make him look like a rabbit already!

3. He has really long front teeth.

4. Don't forget his fluffy tail.

# Horse

Horses can be many different colors. This one is brown and black.

Horses eat grass and hay.

Horses have long legs. They can run fast.

A horse's foot is called a hoof.

FUN FACTS ● FUN FACTS ● FUN FACTS ● FUN FACTS ● FUN FACTS

A horse can go to sleep standing up or lying down.

1. Draw this curvy shape.

2. Now add his face and two legs.

3. Make him stand on three legs.

4. Color him brown. Give him a long tail.

# Tortoise

This tortoise has a hard shell.

She can hide her head and legs inside her shell.

She digs a nest with her back legs.

Tortoises eat grass, leaves, flowers and fruit.

FUN FACTS ● FUN FACTS ● FUN FACTS ● FUN FACTS ● FUN FACTS

Tortoises live for a very long time.
Some live more than 150 years!

1. Here's her shell. Everything's inside!

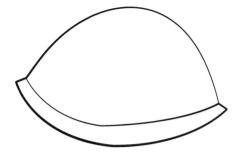

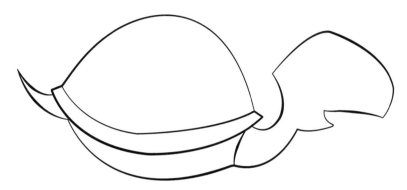

2. She's put her head and tail out.

3. And last come her legs.

4. Her shell has a special pattern on it.

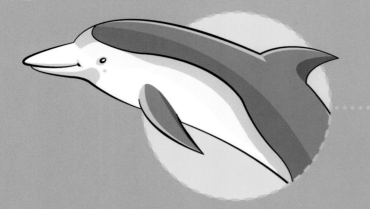

Draw this friendly dolphin leaping from the water.

Crabs have the perfect claws for pinching!

Draw this shark - if you dare...

This stingray looks very happy!

# SEA CREATURES

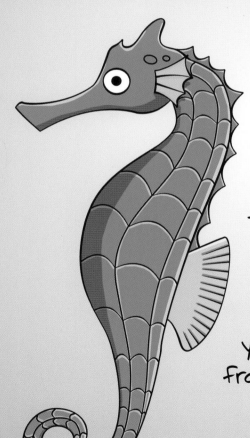

The sea is filled with all sorts of cool creatures for you to recreate on your drawing pad. From huge killer whales to tiny seahorses - you won't be short of inspiration from the underwater world!

# Killer whale

This killer whale has a black body with white patches.

He has a fin on his back.

He has sharp teeth. He eats fish, birds, and sea lions.

His tail moves up and down when he swims.

FUN FACTS ● FUN FACTS ● FUN FACTS ● FUN FACTS ● FUN FACTS

Killer whales live with their families. There are about 20 killer whales in each group.

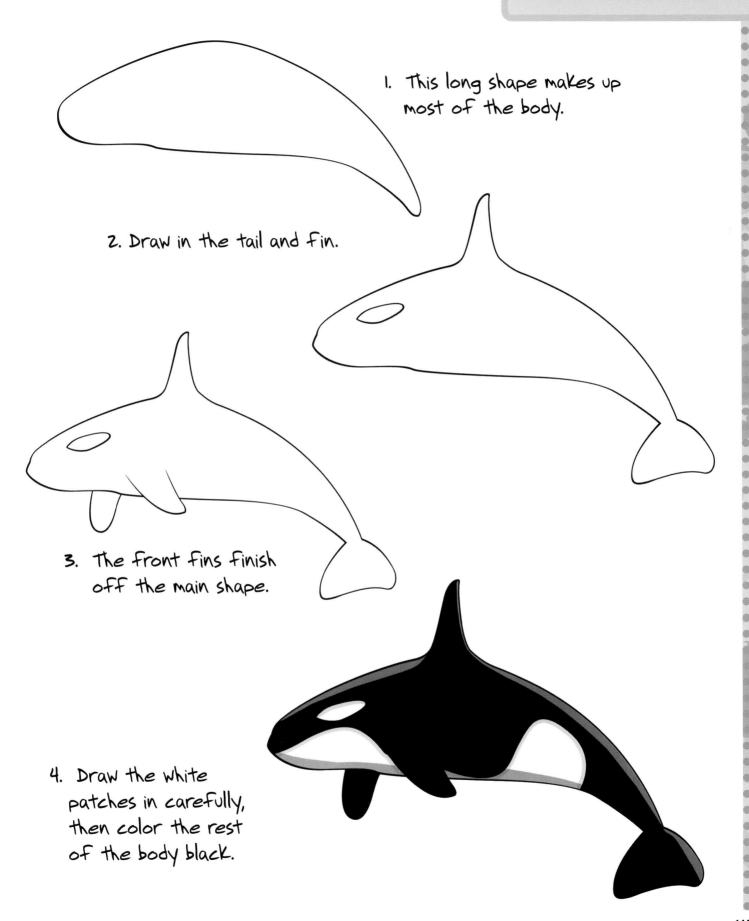

1. This long shape makes up most of the body.

2. Draw in the tail and fin.

3. The front fins finish off the main shape.

4. Draw the white patches in carefully, then color the rest of the body black.

# Clown Fish

This clown fish lives in warm seas.

He is brightly colored, with orange and white stripes.

He is about 3 inches (8 centimeters) long.

He has a special slime on his body. The slime keeps him from getting stung by sea anemones.

FUN FACTS ● FUN FACTS ● FUN FACTS ● FUN FACTS ● FUN FACTS

Clown fish look after their eggs until the babies hatch out.

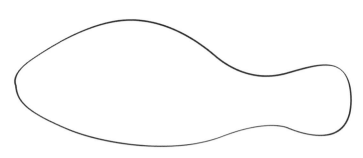

1. Begin with this fishy body shape.

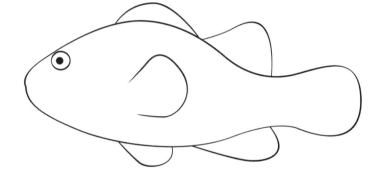

2. Add the fins and an eye.

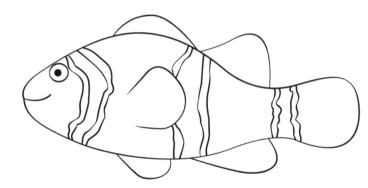

3. Draw some wavy lines for the stripes.

4. Draw some extra, thinner lines on the fins. Then color your fish in.

# Seahorse

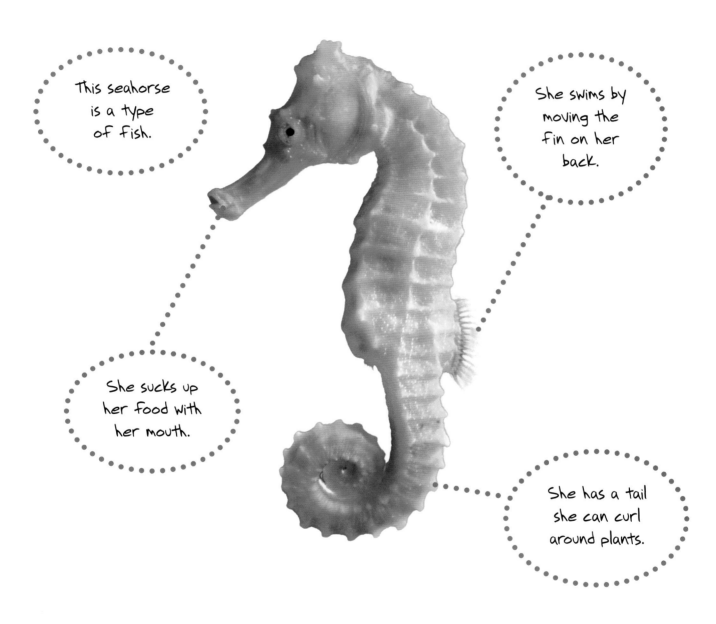

This seahorse is a type of fish.

She swims by moving the fin on her back.

She sucks up her food with her mouth.

She has a tail she can curl around plants.

FUN FACTS ● FUN FACTS ● FUN FACTS ● FUN FACTS ● FUN FACTS

The mother seahorse gives her eggs to the father seahorse. He looks after the eggs until the babies hatch.

1. This curved shape makes up the body.

2. Add the head and the curly tail.

3. Next, draw fins on the head and the back.

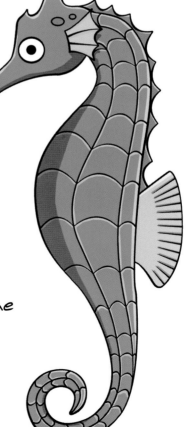

4. Don't forget the spiky mane down the seahorse's neck.

# Shark

He has very sharp teeth. He kills other animals for food.

This shark is called a gray reef shark.

He can smell other animals from far away.

He uses fins to help him swim through the water.

FUN FACTS ● FUN FACTS ● FUN FACTS ● FUN FACTS ● FUN FACTS

The biggest fish in the ocean is the whale shark. It's longer than a bus!

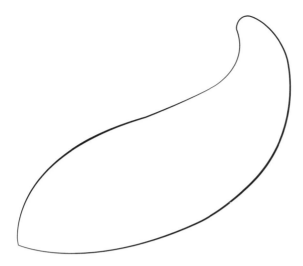

1. Make the body curvy.

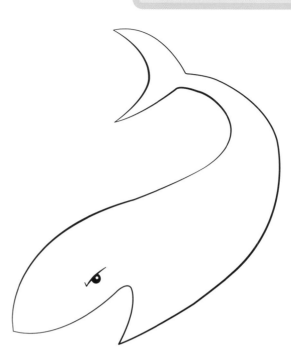

2. Give him a big mouth and an angry eye.

3. The fins and tail are pointed.

4. Finish him off with sharp teeth.

# Dolphin

A dolphin's shape helps him to swim fast.

The dolphin is a playful animal. He jumps through the waves for fun.

Dolphins swim together in groups. The groups are called pods.

He has small, sharp teeth.

FUN FACTS ● FUN FACTS ● FUN FACTS ● FUN FACTS ● FUN FACTS

Dolphins like to talk to each other. They make clicking and whistling sounds.

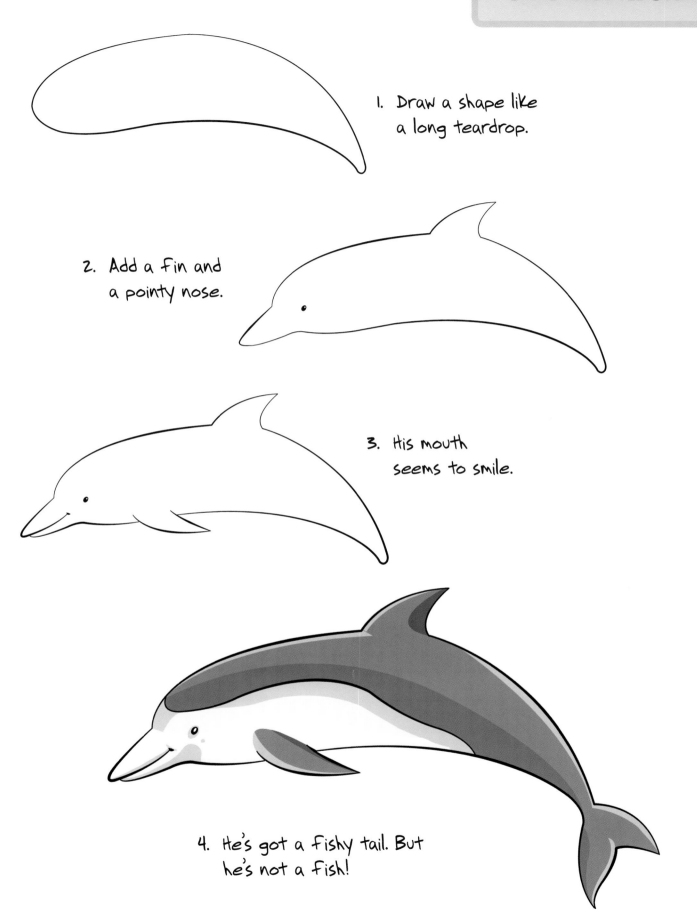

1. Draw a shape like a long teardrop.

2. Add a fin and a pointy nose.

3. His mouth seems to smile.

4. He's got a fishy tail. But he's not a fish!

# Crab

This crab has eight legs and two claws.

She has a hard shell.

She walks sideways.

If she loses a leg, she can grow it back.

FUN FACTS ● FUN FACTS ● FUN FACTS ● FUN FACTS ● FUN FACTS

The smallest crab is only the size of a pea. The largest crab is 12 feet (3.7 meters) wide.

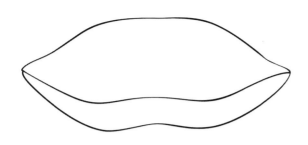

1. Draw a shape that looks like a pair of lips.

2. Add some eyes and two big snapping claws.

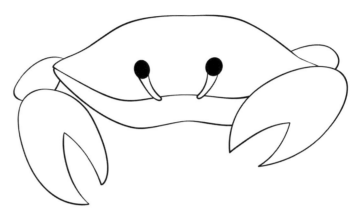

3. Draw four back legs. You can't see all of the crab's legs in this picture.

4. Use orange and brown to finish off your picture.

# Stingray

This stingray has a large, flat body.

He swims by flapping his sides. It looks a bit like a bird flying.

His eyes are on top of his head but his mouth and nose are underneath.

He has a poisonous spine on his tail.

FUN FACTS ● FUN FACTS ● FUN FACTS ● FUN FACTS ● FUN FACTS

Stingrays live at the bottom of the sea. They hide on the sea floor if they are in danger.

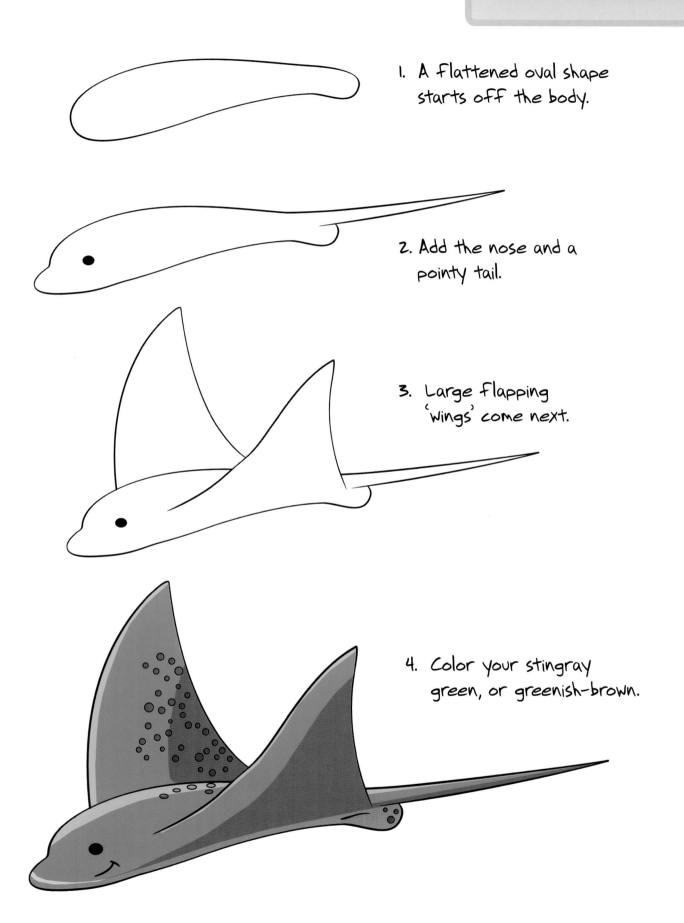

1. A flattened oval shape starts off the body.

2. Add the nose and a pointy tail.

3. Large flapping 'wings' come next.

4. Color your stingray green, or greenish-brown.